BLUE DRAGON, WHITE TIGER

BLUE DRAGON, WHITE TIGER

Verses for Refining the Golden Elixir

Chang Sen Feng

*Translated by Shifu Hwang and
Cheney Crow, Ph.D.*

SINGING
DRAGON

LONDON AND PHILADELPHIA

First published in 2013
by Singing Dragon
an imprint of Jessica Kingsley Publishers
116 Pentonville Road
London N1 9JB, UK
and
400 Market Street, Suite 400
Philadelphia, PA 19106, USA

www.singingdragon.com

Library of Congress Cataloging in Publication Data
A CIP catalog record for this book is available from the Library of Congress

British Library Cataloguing in Publication Data
A CIP catalogue record for this book is available from the British Library

ISBN 978 1 84819 115 0
eISBN 978 0 85701 096 4

Printed and bound in Great Britain

TRANSLATOR'S NOTE

An unusual tantric guidebook, this work was written during the Tang dynasty. It documents a sexual tantra the author claims had been practiced by kings for several dynasties, but lost popularity as Taoist monks discarded sexual practices in favor of more asceticism. Chang Sen Feng's orthodox peers, who favored asceticism, were enraged to learn that he had adopted this practice. They believed sexual practice would propagate evil, and that public knowledge of it would sully the reputation of Taoism. It was decided that Chang Sen Feng should be pursued and killed. According to legend, he was last seen on the edge of a precipice, where, clasping his text to his chest, Chang Sen Feng proclaimed the sincerity of his practice and begged for mercy and understanding.

For almost seven hundred years Chang Sen Feng's text vanished from circulation, yet word of his practice continued to circulate among Taoist monks. The text was rediscovered during the Ming dynasty by Jie Yi Tze. The current translation is based on a 1969 Chinese printing of his publication, called San Feng Dan Jiu, *The Secret Words of Internal Alchemy by Chang Sen Feng*.

In the text, Chang Sen Feng prescribes the methods for preparing oneself to pursue the Tao: developing a foundation for spiritual practice, choosing the physical setting for the practice, using precise techniques for choosing consorts, and astrologically determining the correct moment for practice. Cloaked in metaphor, the techniques and attendant virtues of the practices are presented in poetry and in prose, with explanatory commentaries. Chang Sen Feng refers to the practitioner and his consort with varied images: Blue Dragons and White Tigers; wind and fire; Heaven and Earth.

In addition to his careful description of the methods of practice, the author gives direct warnings to anyone who might choose a more lax interpretation of this practice, and strongly iterates the need for discipline and rigor in the preliminary, intermediate, and advanced phases of this practice. He insists that this practice, like all sexual tantra, be pursued strictly for the spiritual advancement of the practitioner, and undertaken only once desire and attachment for a consort have been overcome.

He carefully underscores the importance of avoiding the inherent difficulties of such endeavors, and claims the ultimate benefits of successful practice are longevity and the completion of internal alchemy, the gradual emergence and alignment of the self in the Tao.

In our translation, respecting the integrity and density of the text occasionally makes it obscure to non-initiates. A few suggested interpretations of our own are set between square brackets within the text. Parentheses are those of the author.

The reader will note that the practice focuses on the spiritual advancement of the male practitioner, with no mention of the female except as a consort. The consorts are well treated and educated by the practitioner's group. Our next translation will be of a very early text written by a woman about spiritual practice.

Cheney Crow, Ph.D.
May 2012

TRANSLATOR'S INTRODUCTION

I N ITS ORIGINAL form, the Taoist faith was focused on reverence for nature and the belief that the universe is a spiritual entity. The writings of Lao Tze, Lieh Tze, and Chung Tze express this belief. As Taoist thought evolved, the philosophy of the Yin-Yang theory of Wu-Shin (Five Elements) and Ba-Kua (Eight Hexagrams) were also adopted. Over time, more ideas of the Yin-Yang school and Confucius's ethical philosophy were assimilated: non-action—not interfering with or trying to control fate—and the conviction that life and death are forms of change. During the Han dynasty a new belief evolved: that through study and spiritual practice, humans could reach the level of the immortal, supernatural world.

This concept, the basis of the Taoist religion, may have evolved as a response to the social climate in China during the Chin and Han dynasties, which were characterized by chaos, insecurity, and repression. For people wishing to escape oppression, spiritual training offers a source of hope. In addition to the possibility of attaining the immortal body, Taoist training held the promise of gaining power over one's human problems of birth, sickness, aging, and death. Through rigorous practice called alchemy, both internal and external, a Taoist could transcend his lifetime and become a god.

External alchemy

Secret arts of alchemy were developed, with "elixirs" whose potency could change the course of fate. The elixirs were derived by systematic experimentation with herbs, minerals, and a special diet, not just the simple five grains earlier Taoists preferred.

Pure mineral substances were introduced, and Taoists added cinnabar, mirabilitum, talcum, realgar, blue sky stone, sulphur, and other ingredients to their elixirs. Because heat was used in preparing the elixirs, the preparation process was called the Art of Forging the Elixir. Thirteen categories were assigned to methods of "forging":

Flying—forging by evaporating.

Overwhelming—vaporizing into a gaseous state.

Dying—decomposition.

Adding Particles—adding small amount of substance to a large mass, creating a chemical reaction.

Making a Gate—combining the reactive substances in a sealed container.

Nourishing—using gentle fire to heat a substance slowly.

Cooking—adding water and increasing the heat.

Forging—manually refining a substance.

Enforcing—enhancing or increasing the speed of reaction.

Arranging—putting a substance into the vessel for alchemy.

Raining—pouring out the liquid.

Securing—sealing the reacted liquid in a vessel.

Making Six and One Mud—using seven different substances in the chemical reaction. The reaction process was called Seven Returning, its result: the Fire Feats. The final product was called the Immortal Elixir.

Many serious practitioners died after ingesting the elixirs they forged. Throughout the Han and Soon dynasties, these experiments continued, and more practitioners succumbed to their own potions. Serious doubts emerged about whether the toxicity of the elixirs developed for external alchemy could be counteracted or overcome.

Internal alchemy

The choice was made to abandon the use of potentially lethal chemicals, and Taoists turned their focus instead to the "three treasures of the human body": the practices of Jin, the essence of body; Qi, the energy flow; and Sen, the spirit. Thus began the development of techniques of internal alchemy. The Qigong practice, focusing on the breath, was developed, using many technical terms from external alchemy. When, during the Soon dynasty, Taoism became the national religion, the art of internal alchemy enjoyed great prosperity.

Throughout the Soon and Yuan dynasties, the Chuen Zen school was famous for its teachings. A recluse in the Huan Mountain named Lu Dong Bin taught the techniques of Jin, Qi and Sen, and the great master Chang Zi Yang taught internal alchemy.

The art of internal alchemy emphasized training the mind and purifying the body through rigorous practice. Its theories were rooted in three early philosophies—of Lao Tze on the Tao, the original essence; of Chang Zi, on transformation; and on the Yin-Yang school's theory of change, based on the rotation of the five elements. The goal of internal alchemy was to overcome death, to attain the immortal body through self-transformation, always in strict obedience to Taoist principles.

Sexual internal alchemy

In the effort to transform internal energies, sexual practices were explored. The idea of harnessing the enormous power of sexual energy as a spiritual vehicle led to the development of practices involving sexual contact. Achieving the extreme discipline required for sexual contact without ejaculation was considered highly spiritual. This became the basis of many practices involving the use of single or even multiple female consorts.

Both "contact" and "non-contact" practices evolved. In "non-contact" practices, neither the man nor the woman disrobed or allowed their emotions to be aroused. They merged their separate Qi into one. In contact practices, the man had to develop his own discipline before he could learn to "collect" energy from a consort.

The practices in this text

Chang Sen Feng, the author of this text, practiced and taught both kinds of sexual alchemy ("contact" and "non-contact"). I encourage you, as he does, to consider these practices with serious intent, and respect for the discipline they require.

Shifu Hwang
May 2012

CONTENTS

Part III The Secrets of Collecting Truth

Part IV The Way of Gathering the Truth

PREFACE

THE TAO MAY be manifest at three different levels [the Tao of Heaven, the Tao of Earth, and Tao of Man]. Each practitioner begins by approaching the fundamental one. The deities may be classified into five ranks. To achieve his initial goal, the practitioner must forego all his animal propensities. All achievement begins with the building of one's foundation. Once this is achieved, the practitioner may begin work on refining his character. Over time he may acquire the ability to receive the potion and blend it into his energy system. Even if a practitioner does not reach the level of conceiving an immortal fetus, he can extend his lifespan and live happily in the world. The practitioner must devote himself entirely to learning the doctrine of the Tao, which has been studied for centuries, and he must put this doctrine into practice. Only by doing this can he acquire the ability to reach the Tao. For practitioners who have studied other arts—separating the soul in sitting, ceasing life in standing, rebirth in planning, occupying the body of another person—if they wish to compare any other practice to the beauty of this Tao, they will find a distance between the two as great as the distance between Heaven and Earth. The followers of this doctrine will be beyond communication with other believers.

It is claimed that the ultimate Tao which preceded all existence, spread the heavens in their span, formed the

Earth, and established the first being, will propagate. With respect for this greatness, whoever wishes to implement the principles of the Tao must begin with all sincerity, maintain stillness, and act with humility and perseverance. At the moment of death, this practice will enable the practitioner to restore himself to vitality and enter the timeless state of chaos of the primordial ages. Merging with the Tao, he will transcend the experience of ordinary people and enter the realm of the sages. His brightness and beauty will be like the sun and the moon; his achievement will illuminate the darkness of antiquity and guide the way to the future. The Tao is almost imperceptible, yet nothing in existence can survive even a moment without it. One cannot be separated from the Tao for even a moment; if it can be left behind, this is not the Tao.

In ancient times, our holy emperor Shien Yun (Hwang Ti) forged his sword using nine consorts, and achieved the goal of ascending to Heaven. The emperor Tong Hwa nourished his three essences and reached the Tao. In Taoism, a distinction is made between Southern and Northern schools; all of its doctrines enlighten Eastern and Western believers. More than ten thousand individual practitioners have achieved the goal of ascending to Heaven. More than eight hundred practitioners have ascended to Heaven with their families. Innumerable practitioners have transformed their bodily forms and changed countenances. In each dynasty there have been practitioners who have achieved delivery of the holy baby and have decomposed their original bodies. All these practitioners have set their souls free through orthodox Taoist art. They used no evil practices to achieve their goals.

If there is no master to pass on the instructions, how can a practitioner achieve such beauty of the body and spirit? I have studied various scriptures of internal alchemy, and I know that in the world of humans and immortals, the way of the Golden Elixir is the best art for attaining the level of a deity. This art is little known in the current generation.

If, as a practitioner, you can truly understand the subtle and precise techniques, you have inherited the root of spirit and the bones of the Tao. Your inheritance of this understanding originates from due cause, which you have benefitted from in previous lifetimes. However, even without such inheritance some of you may gradually accumulate the necessary conditions to complete your goals. Those who lack the financial means for the practice of internal alchemy cannot achieve these feats. As Taoists who practice internal alchemy, when we hear this we can have no regrets; neither can we show anger. If you have the good fortune to meet an enlightened teacher who is willing to teach you the ways of practice, you should begin learning as soon as possible. So that your progress may be rapid, you must invest all your sincerity and energy in this endeavor. If you wish to complete the double practice (Hsin and Ming, intrinsic nature and vital force) you must perform good deeds and respect moral behavior. As you progress from the lowest point to the vortex, from initiation to consummation, you must continually increase your effort and courage. In this way you may reach your goals in countable days. When you can achieve detachment from the desires of visual and physical attraction, you will be able to fortify and protect your unlimited cultivated body. The result is beautiful.

Every man has inherited the Tao, which is inherently good. Once you can capture and control your changes of Yin and Yang, you will be able to lengthen your lifespan until it is as long as Heaven and Earth. Embracing the Tao and respecting its etiquette, you come to my school to learn. As long as your mind is sincere, my teachings cannot lead you astray. Therefore, with my unadorned words I offer this teaching to those who are interested in my school. The seven techniques that follow the principle of the orthodox Tao, from the book *Gin Dan Jie Yao* (*The Brief Verses on the Art of the Golden Elixir*). All of these techniques are given separate titles, and explanations follow each one. Through study and careful reflection on this text, you will come to understand the subtle theories. One day, when you fully comprehend the theory, you will spontaneously feel all the sensations in your body. The moment you understand the theory, your mind will begin to transform. Your countenance will become quiet and calm, and your soul will gradually blend with the Tao. Once you receive the Tao, you will become one with it forever. The path of immortality is reached.

However, if ever you lose control, or lose restraint of your passion in breathing, ten thousand different sensations may occur that are not in accordance with the Tao. Should this come to pass, you will be unable to achieve the true Tao, and the way to becoming immortal will be unreachable. You must begin with a pious mind, and proceed to the end carefully. Only in this way will you achieve your goal.

Chang Sen Feng

Part I

Preparation of the Mind

Cultivating the Qi Through Sole Breathing

———— ※ ————

How great is the mystical mother who emits the primordial Qi from her center, the bellows! The mother comes from infinite time and space (Wu Ji). How great are Yin and Yang, her successors, the two elements from which the seventh and eighth varieties can emerge! Yet, even with great striving, not all beings who seek blessing from Heaven can attain this blessing. Although immortals in Heaven and humans hold the same view of all sentient beings, the paths of humans and immortals are separate. Months and years pass by like flowing water. Sunrise and sunset exchange their scenes in the blink of an eye. The world of the dead and the world of the living are separate, alas! Winding roads are easy to follow; the straight path is hard to find. If the way of man has not been cultivated, the way of immortals will be far, far away.

The man who devotes himself to seeking the absolute Tao must strive for this. He can progress on the mystical path if he practices every day, morning and evening. He must reduce his food intake, wear loose clothing, and sit in a quiet chamber [room] holding his hands in the shape of a heart with his heels touching the Di Fu (the top of the thighs). His tongue touches the upper palate, his lips and teeth are lightly clenched. He adjusts his breath so it is gentle, as soft as cotton, and it flows through the soles of his feet. His spirit and breath enter and exit in unison. He quietly maintains control of his mind and body. His heart is calm and his outer appearance is tranquil. With all his thoughts focused on his center, all attractions are discarded. He closes the four doors of the chamber and with his mind's eye he observes his inward body. He visualizes a pearl the size of a kernel of corn, in the Hwang Tin (Yellow Palace), in the middle Dan Tien. Then he arranges the sun of his character at the Li Wan, and the moon of the bodily essence at the Dan Fu (the Mansion of Elixirs, the middle Dan Tien). He tries to make his breath as even and as gentle as possible, he concentrates his spirit, then holds his breath for a long time. He rests in this natural ambience. Then he slowly swallows down his true Qi, and gradually sends it to his Dan Tien (lower Dan Tien). His Qi surges up from the origin of the bodily essence, follows the channel of the Du meridian, passes through the Wei Lu and rises to the Li Wan. There it arouses the origin of character and follows the channel of the Ren meridian and flows into the Min Tang (Bright Hall, the third Dan Tien) before falling into the Dan Fu. The Qi circulates like a wheel turning on the upper, middle, and lower three Dan Tiens.

In the practitioner's back the Qi rises and in his front it moves downward. It flows this way continuously. The practitioner's mind remains as still as clear water, and his body as transparent as a teapot made of ice. He contracts his anus, raises his bowels and breathes slowly through the soles of his feet. If the practitioner feels his breathing is too fast, he can slowly swallow down his saliva to help slow down his breath. If he feels drowsy at times, visualization techniques can be effective. He must concentrate from his first breath, gradually developing this into a hundred, then a thousand breaths. Then he can tirelessly breathe like this as many times as there are stars in the heavens. At this stage he will be able to experience the mystical effects of his training.

The practitioner must become proficient at this training first. If he cannot develop the practice of Sole Breathing, and detach himself from outside attractions, all his actions are just time wasted. Developing the difficult practice of Sole Breathing is the practitioner's first task.

Accumulating Qi to Open the Gate

———— ❊ ————

THIS PRACTICE BEGINS with the same initial procedure as the practice of Sole Breathing. The practitioner folds his hands and intertwines his fingers, focusing his mind at the Yu Fu (Jade Mansion, the middle Dan Tien). He concentrates on gathering his Qi, slows down all his bodily functions and enters the state of tranquility. First, he visualizes the Qi flowing in through the Yong Chuan acupoint of his left foot (Bubbling acupoint, Kidney 1). Gradually the Qi rises to his knees and thighs, and passes over the three gates, reaching the Ni Wan and then it falls slowly into the Yuan Hai (Original Sea, the lower Dan Tien). Once again, the Qi flows in through the Yong Chuan of the right foot, then rises and falls along the right side of the body. This mirrors the purpose and function of the left side.

Next, the Qi circulates four times on the right and the left sides. Then it enters through two acupoints simultaneously (right and left Yong Chuan acupoints) and circulates once more. Nine consecutive circulations make one Complete Circulation. The practitioner visualizes lifting up his bowels, slows down his Sole Breathing and does nine Complete Qi Circulations, a total of eighty-one. This practice should help the Qi circulate naturally by clearing obstructions from the gates of the meridians. If after this practice he still cannot open the gates to his meridians, the practitioner can try using the Wu Jiu (internal force, the martial artists' Qigong) to guide his Qi circulation.

To begin the Wu Jiu, the practitioner assumes the "Lion Leaning Back" sitting posture, opens his eyes and inhales three times. The Qi will smoothly pass through the lower gate. When he feels the Qi rise to the level of his elbow, he swallows his saliva. Next he shrugs his shoulders, so the Qi will be drawn up to the Ni Wan. The practitioner completes the exercises of the Great Water Mill (Large Heaven Circulation). Then he shakes his Kun Lun (Bladder 60), rubs his abdomen for a count of eighty-one times. He rubs his head and face twenty-four times. When this is done, he pats the crown of his head three times and rotates his eyes eight times. He concentrates his mind and clenches his teeth together four or six times.

Throughout the Wu Jiu, the practitioner must raise his bowels, and control his breath. Afterwards, he must stir his saliva with his tongue and swallow one-third of it. Then he can shake his body and stand up. He shakes his body, first the left side then the right side, nine times. This sequence is called the Action technique. The practitioner can blend it with the Still technique by alternately using one, then the other. By repeating these two practices without interruption, the practitioner will have a better chance of achieving his cultivation. For the superior practitioner, it will take approximately three days and nights to open his meridians' gates. For a middle quality practitioner it will take fourteen days to achieve this. The inferior practitioner will spend a month practicing before his gates will open. For a lazy person, this may take one hundred days. If the practitioner feels an ache in his spine, he can slow down the practice. On sunny and hot days, the practitioner may exhale and undertake the Water Mill exercise more frequently. If the practitioner is diligent in this practice, he will not suffer from any kind of sickness. He will feel wind generated in his Li Wan, and a steaming sensation in the Qi of the kidney. After experiencing this sensation, the practitioner can feel the fragrance in his Magpie Bridge (where the tongue touches the palate, in the shape of a bridge), and sweet dew drips down. If the practitioner is unable to experience this sensation, his practice must be incorrect. If he can't open his gates with this method, how can he guide his Qi as it rises and falls? How can he cultivate his character to match his body's essence?

CULTIVATING THE BODY'S ESSENCE WITH JADE FLUID

—— ⁂ ——

THE PROCEDURE FOR transforming the jade fluid into an elixir is more exciting than the last instruction. It relies on using the gold fluid to refine the ordinary lid [sexual fluids]. For this, the practitioner must learn the art of Forging the Sword, and the art of Grafting, after which he can attain an immortal lifespan of ten thousand years. To carry out this procedure, three or five trivets [consorts, maidens] must be chosen. Each of them should not be over sixteen or seventeen years old—fourteen is the best. Their appearance should be smooth, and unblemished, like a blossoming flower. They should be mature enough to produce seeds; it is inappropriate to select a trivet who has not reached puberty. The practitioner and consort remain in a quiet chamber, day and night, facing each other in a seated position. Both expose their natural forms, then proceed to strike the bamboo and raise the plumet. Next they strum the lute [masturbation], producing harmonious sounds. Each sequence is repeated three times. Gradually, the two persons' emotions blend into union. The practitioner's "intention to conquer" arises. However, he must not allow his desire to become a raging current. Slowly he sends his dragon to enter the cave. Lightly he holds his sword and returns it to its sheath. When the head of the turtle moves forward one inch, the practitioner must exhale, retaining about thirty to fifty percent of his breath. He draws up his bowels at this time, places his hands at his waist, shrugs his shoulders, and retracts his neck. Silently he visualizes two currents of air, red and white, rising up and slowly mounting into the great sky of the void, with which they blend and appear as the great mass of a dark wheel. It has bright luster and shines in the mystical mother.

After this moment, the practitioner closes his eyes and focuses his mind on Hwang Tin (the Yellow Palace, the middle Dan Tien). He visualizes the luster illuminating the Gate of Heaven (the crown of the head), and then tries to turn his eyes upward, toward the mystical valley. The practitioner is oblivious to the existence of his body and his partner; his emotions and the scene are both beyond his awareness. The practitioner's sweet dew gradually forms, and drips into his Dan Tien. The body is quiet and motionless throughout the excitement, and the dew is generated. This is the body's essence intertwined with the breath. The spirit is not yet engaged. The dragon's intercourse with the tiger is the art of setting up the stove and the trivet. The next step of the procedure is the cooking. This is also the art of adjusting the essence of Yin and Yang. Thus the practice goes: the upper corner moon changes into the lower corner moon, and then the full moon. The practitioner performs both the Action and Tranquil techniques four times a day. Following these instructions step by step, and repeating them from the beginning to the end, he will complete the practice of Heaven Circulation. The practitioner maneuvers his Qi skillfully to circulate through his three meridian gates. The two Chis of his Yin and Yang blend into a single unit. When he reaches this level, the practitioner has completed the art of intertwining his spirit with his breath, without engaging the essence of his body. Next, he activates the bellows in harmony with his spirit. He continually fans the fire, and slowly blows into it with the bellows. He draws the wind from the bottom to the top at will. He sends in his organ with a slow exhalation, and draws it back with a strong, brief inhalation.

He fans his arms thirty-six times, then stops and remains still. Once more he draws up his chest, lightly, twenty-four times and swallows up his breath with his saliva. Once again he rubs his belly sixteen times. He repeats this technique three times. Each movement requires six clockwise circles, then six counterclockwise circles. After he completes this practice, the practitioner begins the Tranquil technique. For this, he lets the Qi circulate nine times through the three meridian gates of his back. If he is worried that he has not drawn up his Qi, the practitioner can use three techniques from martial arts, facing the stove, to forge his sword, practicing four times during the day and night. In the tranquil state, the practitioner guides his Qi; in the action state, he uses the martial arts techniques. By practicing continuously, he can achieve great effectiveness.

When he meets the coming of the Tide and the coming out of the moon from the west, he can fan his arms and collect the potion. Within a quarter of an hour, he can receive the potion three or four times.

Through this practice he can lengthen his lifespan to two or three hundred years. This practice can lead the practitioner to experience fascinating results. The practitioner should constantly drink the immortal wine, avoiding plucking the flower which is on the verge of decay. Easily he strums the stringless lute, and slowly lets the holeless flute be blown. This art is so subtle and marvelous. Hasty practice, however, can bring only harm, not benefit, to the practitioner. The way of the Golden Elixir is achieved through the union of two body forms.

The effectiveness of the jade fluid cannot be complete without this practice.

Therefore, it is said "To collect the medicine is easy; to cultivate the body's essence is very difficult." The practitioner must train his character to be alert and develop spiritual harmony, detaching his mind from worldly affairs, and achieving internal stability. The practice can be completed in one hundred days. Its results surpass the art of Heaven Circulation, and all other forms of internal alchemy. No other internal alchemy can be superior to this. The art of revitalizing, through grafting life energy, can be completed through this practice. If the practitioner is courageous and diligent, he can easily achieve this goal. If, on the contrary, he is lazy and sluggish, he can achieve almost nothing. This art is the most important device for completing the cultivation of the bodily essence using the jade fluid, and the only method of Forging the Sword with the gold water.

Part II

Preparing the Practice

GATHERING THE WEALTH TO CULTIVATE THE PRACTICE

--- ⁂ ---

WEALTH MUST BE acquired from an untainted source. An abundance of wealth must be available, enough so that one never has to worry about shortage of funds. If the money is from an impure source, the practitioner will inherit its negative karma, so one must be careful in choosing his source of money.

SELECTING THE PLACE FOR PRACTICE

WITH THE ASSISTANCE of a powerful and wealthy family, a practitioner can live outside of a city. He must choose carefully. If he chooses a family that has power, but not wealth, there will be no resources to sustain the tremendous cost of establishing and carrying out the practice. If he chooses assistance from a family that has wealth, but no power, he may be vulnerable to persecution. Wealth provides him the choice to live in the country, where the soil is red or yellow. There should be no ancient tombs or cemeteries on the land. The land should have natural springs, and the neighbors should be kind. The land on which the house is built should be uncontaminated by animal droppings or other animal waste. The land should have a good view of mountains and beautiful rivers. It should be considered an auspicious place. These features are essential to the development of good practice, so the practitioner must be very serious in his choice of place.

Choosing the Companions

❋

CHOOSING ONLY AMONG people whose spiritual pursuits are the same as his, a practitioner should select companions with whom he can develop lifelong relationships. The companions must be pure and harmonious in character. They must possess the necessary qualities of loyalty, fidelity, friendship, and brotherhood. Companions of this sort can help and support each other in their practice. This is essential to diligent practice and prevention of accidents. At the moment of completion of achieving internal alchemy, the practitioner will act like a drunkard and an idiot. Incapacitated by this state, he must entrust his life totally to the care of his fellow practitioners and servants, without whose protection he may even risk death.

Building the Chambers for Practice

———— ※ ————

T HE CHAMBERS USED for this practice are part of the house of internal alchemy. It should be divided into three sections, the first of which is a front section with a large living area and a courtyard. To the left and right of the living area should be two chambers. In the second section, the middle area, should be an activity room, with three adjoining rooms on the left and right: the rooms on the left side are for the kitchen, those on the right for storage. The activity room should also have space to store supplies. In the kitchen there should be a shrine to the Heavenly General to guard those who are fasting, and by his presence remind them to maintain their fast. The third section should have three rooms. The central room must have a shrine to the Taoist grand masters, five generations of Taoist masters, seven accomplished masters, and sixteen Heavenly Generals. On the table where the shrine rests should be a bowl of clean water, incense, fresh flowers, several reliquaries, an adjustable clock to keep time properly, and all the Taoist scriptures so that the Taoists may consult and read from these books morning and evening. The rooms to the left and the right of the central room are for the guards to live in. Their rooms should be separated from the central room. Only a hole about one square meter in size should be left through which food may be passed into the central room for the practitioners. Each section has three rooms, the back, the middle, and the front sections. The three rooms on the East side are for the Blue Dragons, the practitioners. The three rooms on the west side are for White Tigers, those consorts chosen for the practice. In the middle are the grand master's shrines. Facing the direction of twelve o'clock noon, on the left side is the practice room and on the right side is a leisure room. The windows and the tables should be wiped clean, and high walls should surround all the four sides of the structure, so that no one can see inside. Many flowers should be planted, and a fence should enclose and protect them. Cranes and deer should be raised there for the amusement of the practitioners. The garden is for the girls to enjoy.

CHOOSING CONSORTS

───────── ❋ ─────────

HERE THE CONSORTS* are true dragons and true tigers. The first step in choosing appropriate consorts is to find pretty-faced young girls. Pretty-faced refers to clean lines in the eyebrows, and clear and graceful eyes. Their lips are red and their teeth are beautiful and white. There are three classes of consort: the lowest class includes those of the ages five-five (twenty-five years old), three-eight (twenty-four), and three-seven (twenty-one). Despite their age, these older consorts can still be used for practice. They are used to help enhance the fire, and to nourish the weakness of the dragons. The middle class of consorts includes the ages five-four (twenty years old), two-nine (eighteen), and two-eight (sixteen), pretty-faced girls who have reached puberty but have not experienced the encounter of Yin and Yang [intercourse], and have not yet given birth, whose water wheel [maidenhead] has not been broken. As consorts these women can enhance the practitioner's life and strengthen his body. Through this practice, the practitioner can attain the initial deity form of the human being. The seven-seven consorts (fourteen years old) are the top class, the best medicine supply. These girls are like the original formless essence of life. Their characters have the purity of the moon in Heaven. As consorts they are called the true White Tigers. The true

───────────────

* The word "consort" literally means "trivet," a three-legged support for a cooking pot, in symbolic reference to the preparation for "cooking" the elixir.

Blue Dragons are two-eight (sixteen years old) dragons, whose sperm has never been lost. These are called true Blue Dragons. Although there are three classes of consort, a single standard must be maintained in their selection. Their bodies must be complete. Their five facial organs should be normal. Their characters should be mild and harmonious. They should show obedience to Heaven, Earth, and the gods. They should never envy their superiors. Each one chosen must meet this standard. No potential consort who shows signs of any of these ten problems [see pages 45–6] may be selected.

TESTING THE QUALITY OF THE CONSORT

———— ❊ ————

THE CONSORT MAY be of three different qualities. Those in the first, or top class, are called the gold consorts. The second-class consorts are called fire consorts, and the third class are called water consorts. What are the qualities of a gold consort? She is seven-seven (fourteen years old), and can be as valuable as gold. The girl grows for five thousand and forty-eight days, or fourteen years, which Buddhists called one treasure. At this age her heavenly flowers [menses] are coming, and her yellow tunnel is constantly open. After the onset of menstruation (Tzen Jin), this consort is a priceless treasure, true gold. The book of *Tzen Jin Gu* (*The Songs of the True Scriptures*) says that for Tzen Jin there was originally no single word that could deliver a multitude of people to Heaven. In *Chao Shih Kao*, the songs of the trigrams of the I Ching, it says seven-seven, White Tiger, and eight-eight, Blue Dragon, can do this. Chen (male) consorts should be entrusted to a virtuous Taoist friend to learn and practice filial piety day and night. In this way they can acquire the conventional manners, and be freed from evil desires. Kuan (female) consorts should be entrusted to an elderly Taoist woman servant. These two [Kuan and Chen consorts] are supreme internal and external medicines, which should not be considered unimportant. After the practitioner collects and refines the essence of this medicine for half an hour, he can attain the level of a heavenly deity.

Who can become a fire consort? Several girls of two-nine (eighteen years old) and two-eight (sixteen years old) may be prepared by three or five Taoist friends who constantly work with them. If a practitioner can produce medicine with them two or three times, his lifespan can extend to several hundred years. If a practitioner regularly uses nine consorts, he can live on Earth forever and be called a human deity.

Who can become a water consort? Girls who are three-seven (twenty-one years old), four-six (twenty-four years old), five-five (twenty-five years old), and three-nine (twenty-seven years old), who have already experienced the game of playing water by Blue Dragon [sexual intercourse] but have not given birth. Their water wheel [maidenhead] (Hu-Tze) has been broken. These girls can be used for nourishing one's Qi, building the foundation [a practice in which one retains vitality through internal alchemy], and Forging the Sword through the method of Jin Chue (metal and water). Women who have any of the five kinds of illnesses or the ten troubles must not be chosen. If, disregarding this warning, a practitioner uses such consorts, his practice will suffer regression rather than advancement. The five illnesses include: Loah (making a snare); Wuen (smelling bad); Gu (getting stuck); Jiao (being a mixture); Mau (having a meridian problem). Loah indicates a woman whose tunnel has a horizontal bone obstructing it. There is difficulty in collecting medicine from such a woman. Wuen indicates a woman whose body smells. The water from her tunnel has an unpleasant odor. Gu is the name for a woman who does not have regular menstruation. Jiao is the name given to women whose voice sounds like the voice of a man, and whose skin is rough to the touch. Such a woman's face is dark and her hair is yellow [light hair was still unknown in China]. She is easily angered and vicious. Her blood and breath are also unclean. Mau is the name for women who have had malaria and irregular menstruation.

There are five illnesses to be avoided in a male consort. These are: Tsen (lethargic), Dai (volatile), Hu (muted), Bai (half), Du (offensive). Tsen is the name for boys whose bodies are small and whose sexual organ cannot become erect. Dai is the name for boys with a hot temper, and whose mind is undiscriminating. These boys are also proud and violent in their behavior. Hu is the name for boys who have acquired knowledge through early sexual experience. Their sperm has lost its vitality. Bai is the name for boys who are neither male nor female, generally called Yin-Yang men. Du is the name for boys whose hair is yellow, whose eyes bulge out, and whose bodies have an unpleasant odor and boils. These boys are frequently ill, and their behavior is deceitful.

CHOOSING THE GOLD CONSORT

———— ※ ————

ONE SHOULD CHOOSE consorts with elegant eyes and graceful eyebrows, and mild and harmonious characters. Their birthdates are also important. The year, month, day, and hour of their birth should not be in opposition to that of the practitioner. The book [unknown reference] says that he who is born between three and five o'clock in the afternoon in a bad year should be matched with persons born between nine and eleven in the morning. Persons born between nine and eleven in the evening should seek out those born between three to five in the morning. Choosing Kuan (female) consorts by outer appearance is obvious—anyone can see which are beautiful and which are ugly. As for their internal medicine, how can we discern whether or not it is good?

This method can be used. Shape a round coin with one-tenth of an ounce of pure gold. With good quality silver, make a silver coin. Bind these two coins together with silk thread, and put them in the mouth of the consort in the evening. One must spend the night with her to watch her until the next morning, when the coins should be removed and inspected. If the gold coin has a dark red color and the silver coin is a red color, this consort is of the best quality. If the gold coin is red colored and the silver coin is shiny, she is the second best quality. Either may be selected. These women have flowers and seeds, medicine and fire, all necessary for the top quality consort. If the gold coin is a pink color and the silver coin is a black color, she is the lowest quality of trivet, for these women do not have flowers, seeds, medicine, or fire. Without these qualities, a woman is unsuitable as a consort, and cannot be selected.

Choosing the Fire Consort

———— ✦ ————

THE METHOD USED to choose a fire consort is quite different from that used to chose a gold consort. In choosing a fire consort, the practitioner uses white cotton paper soaked in alum water and set out to dry. When the paper has dried, the practitioner must put the paper on his navel and cover it with a coin. Then he should use his tongue to touch the tongue of the girl, to arouse her emotions. After this, the girl should sit on top of the coin and the paper, straddling the body of the practitioner as if she were riding a horse. A little while later, the girl should be removed and the paper inspected. If the paper is damp with water, then she is unsuitable as a consort.

A second method can be used for testing the quality of a fire consort. In this method, a wooden bucket is filled to the brim with clean ash. The girl is then instructed to sit on the bucket for an hour. After this time, the girl is removed and the ash is examined. If the surface of the ash has a dip in it, then she is unsuitable as a consort and cannot be used.

Choosing the Water Consort

---　✦　---

THE TEST FOR choosing a water consort is different from the tests for the fire and gold consorts. The consort should be asked the date and time of her menstruation in the previous month, and then be examined on the same date the next month to see if the symptoms are the same. Then an elderly woman servant should be instructed to examine the color. If it is purple or black, and the time is earlier or later, these are symptoms of sickness and the woman should not be used. Only those whose dates and months match for the two consecutive months and whose menstrual color is a brilliant red may be chosen.

CULTIVATING THE BODY'S ESSENCE
AND BUILDING THE FOUNDATION

———————— ※ ————————

M AGICAL POWERS ARE not innate to either immortal deities or Taoist practitioners. Through effort, they must learn to accumulate semen and enhance their Qi, becoming immortally pure. Accumulation means retaining their own essence (semen). Qi can be enhanced by harvesting Qi from other persons' bodies. The Tao must be the guiding principle for any instance of this. Every aspect of this technique is designed for such harvesting.

If the practitioner can study both accumulation and enhancement, he can transform his mind and his surroundings, imitating the action of the atmosphere which reaches both up to Heaven and down to Earth. This practice brings the calm of the void, or emptiness, to his immediate environment. Because of this, his emotions return to their original pure state. It is said that the body has true Yin or Yang, or true husband and wife, that can be experienced through sexual practice. However, one cannot enter the inner chamber, where the medicine can be gathered, if one neglects to first build up a foundation and purge his character of faults. The practitioner must begin by purifying his character. Once this is achieved, collecting the medicine becomes as easy as rotating his own palm.

Building up Qi to Pass the Gate

※

THE HUMAN BODY contains three gates and nine cavities. The three gates are: Wei Lu, at the tailbone; Jia Ji, on both sides of the midpoint of the spine; and Yu Zen, at the base of the skull. These gates and cavities will open up spontaneously when one has built up enough pure Qi. This requires diligent practice. Such diligent practice will also make the body's "Water Mill" operational. The "Water Mill" raises the Qi up the spine, then down the front of the body at the chest, a process which cleanses all the impurities of the Qi. Once the practice is complete, the three gates and the nine cavities will open simultaneously.

EXTENDING THE LIFESPAN BY
SWALLOWING JADE FLUID

———————— ※ ————————

THE PRACTITIONER CAN convert innate Qi to medicine for ascending to Heaven. Qi acquired through training can be used to extend one's lifespan. "When the full moon is over, it will naturally wane. The time of its upper and lower edges should be carefully remembered. When fifteen is over, another fifteen. Fifty-eight plus sixty-two, I count my fingers to count one hundred and twenty." After twenty-two and a half days, it is time for the transmission of the true content of the practice. For this to be accurate, an aged woman servant must make precise calculations of the appropriate time. On the first and the fifteenth days of the lunar cycle, the Qi of metal [the lung] is generated in abundance. As this happens, the woman's water sources fill up approximately one-fifth. Using a white silk ribbon handkerchief one can touch the woman to check the color and smell of her secretion. If the secretion is as clear as pure water, the time is right for practice with this woman.

"When the moon holds the shoulder of the sun, and the sun holds its back, when she exhales I start my inhalation, and guard my center." Facing each other in these conditions, detached from sentimentality, the practitioner can use the potion [woman's water] to purge his own mercury [the Qi in the blood]. Good fortune will result when the Magpie Bridge is built. Throughout this practice, one's mind must remain detached from all the impulses of the body. The practitioner penetrates only one and a third inches, to not overextend. He should request his consort to move slightly three or five times. At all times he should refrain from thinking of the sexual act, focusing his thoughts on the void. As much as possible the practitioner should remain still, in a tranquil state. The eyes of the tiger [consort's vagina] open wide, while the consort's jade pollen [her orgasmic fluids] sprays out. With the head of the dragon still erect and straight, he should drink the Tao Kaui [her fluids].

This first action should last the time it takes four inches of incense to burn. The second encounter should last the time it takes to burn one inch of incense, while the third and fourth should be half as long. The third and fourth time combined should last for the burning of one inch of incense.

When the golden flower totally decays, the practitioner should send the woman away. The blade of the sword [practitioner's erect organ] remains hot as fire while the medicine is transmitted to the practitioner's body. Next the practitioner meditates, making the medicine move up and stay in the Yellow Palace [middle Dan Tien]. He should ascend to nine-nine Heaven immediately so that he can use the Qi of lid [sperm] to match his Qi of mercury [blood]. [This nine-nine means one turn of the Water Mill: a full circulation up the spine and down the front of the body.]

If after this his temperature remains hot, the practitioner should do another one hundred and five Heaven Circulations. This method, called collecting water, should extinguish the fire. This interaction of water and fire lays a foundation for medicine. One can make twenty-five attempts in a period of three hundred hours. This is the secret of the deities' extending their lives. Every part of a sentence [every aspect of one's life] can be used as a technique for mind training. The practitioner should not allow himself to be persuaded to reveal the secret of the heavens even if others offer him a thousand pieces of gold.

Using Gold Water to Forge the Sword

※

THE CONSORT STAYS in the palace of gold water (northwest). The practitioner seeks company from a wood fire (southeast). The tiger [consort] obtains her life source from water (north); the dragon [practitioner] obtains his life source from fire (south). The practitioner carries an invisible sword [consciousness] at his side, with which he has the occasional opportunity to slay evil [wanton thoughts]. There are visible swords on the Blue Dragon to lure the mysterious potion. Motionless in body and in mind, the practitioner diligently carries out his practice. In this way he prepares himself to come to the stove and face the conditions of Forging his Sword. This practice will ensure effective results as long as the learner remains careful and discerning.

RECOVERING THE GOLDEN ELIXIR

———— ❈ ————

ONCE THE MEDITATION chamber is ready and the consort has been prepared, Taoist scriptures and shrines of several deities and thunder gods should be placed in the center of the chamber. On the third day at seven or eight o'clock the Chen [male] and Kuan [female] consorts place their hands on each other's shoulders. The Chen stays on top and the Kuan stays below. The male must not take off his outer garment, and the woman shouldn't loosen her belt. Both remain properly dressed. The aged

yellow woman servant performs all services for them. She strums the lute [woman's organ] and beats the bamboo rod [man's organ] to call the phoenix [woman's arousal] and the turtle [man's arousal], with Heaven and Earth in their proper positions. The Kuan consort uses the heated date [her lips] to constantly feel the Chen's temperature. Her tongue seems moistened with water. Then the practitioner knows the medicine is generating. While her lips are as hot as fire, the practitioner knows the medicine is circulating, and he can use the Harvesting Technique. The practitioner carefully observes her eyebrows. When a bright white glow crosses her forehead, the White Tiger will have already discharged some water. When the water is released, the practitioner carefully observes the bead to see if it shines through the curtain. If it shines through the curtain, and if the moisture reflects light like the scales of a fish, these are symbols of good luck. The practitioner takes off the tiger's undergarments as well as his own. Both of them sit on a three-legged chair, with Earth [woman] on the top and Heaven [man] below. The practitioner breathes using a technique called the Blacksmith's Bellows. He closes his three precious gems: spirit, breath, and essence of semen. He inwardly examines his own mind. His mind must have no desire. He examines his outer bodily form. He is oblivious to his bodily form. Everything in his sight is void. If he cannot become the void, his mind is still tainted by attachment. So, cautious of the potential danger, the practitioner cannot have even the slightest wanton thought. He waits until the water reaches the level of two-tenths. He uses energy which makes his kidney organs function, contracting his anus, to release the Qi of his blood (true mercury) to meet with her potion (water). He remains motionless while he collects the energy from the woman. At the same time, he uses his mind to focus on his great mysterious gate (the lower Dan Tien), to push this energy upwards from the Wei Lu acupoint (tailbone), enter Ni Wan (the brain), passing the Golden Bridge (the tongue touching the palate, the Magpie Bridge), then his energy is stationed at the Yellow Palace (the middle Dan Tien). Using all of his concentration to focus on the flow of the energy, like a hen hatching her eggs, or the dragon holding the pearl in his mouth, the practitioner should not allow his concentration to waver. As soon as he harvests the medicine, he should give thanks to the teachings of his preceptors, and make offerings to the holy mother in Heaven.

[During the aftermath of practice] the practitioner drinks several mouthfuls of peach wine. Then the fire of his physical body should be quenched. This produces a state of drunken oblivion, a condition that lasts for seven days. For sustenance during this time he must rely on his woman servant and the help of his fellow practitioners. When he attains this level, he is already a primary deity. However, when the initial Qi is newly established, his holy fetus (spiritual body) is newly formed, and any kind of fright can cause the loss of this attainment. It is essential that the practitioner be protected during this time.

Selecting the Time for
Heaven Circulation

———— ✳ ————

A FIXED SHI, or two-hour time period, must be chosen for the practice of Heaven Circulation. This shi is not randomly chosen hours of the year or month, but the midnight hour when innate physical conditions occur. If the practitioner seeks to practice the recovery of the Golden Elixir, he must select his hour. He must choose trivets who are thirteen, fifteen, sixteen or seventeen years old. To calculate their age, the practitioner counts from the day they were born. Every day has twelve shi (two-hour periods). Every month has thirty days, and every year twelve months. The days of the leap year should be excluded from this calculation. If the girl is twelve years old, the first year is called tze, and the second year tzo. The third year is called yin, and the fourth, mao. The fifth year is called chen, and the sixth year gi. The seventh year is called wu, the eighth year is called wei. The ninth year is called sen, and the tenth, yo. The eleventh year is called woo and the twelfth year is called hai. These are the years of Heaven Circulation.

To find the correct month for Heaven Circulation, one calculates the thirteen-year-old's age in the first month, and the first month of the seventeen-year-old's age as the tze, and the twelfth month, the hai. These are the months of Heaven Circulation. To find the correct day for Heaven Circulation for the fourteen-year-old, one counts from the first day of the fourteen-year-old's age, practicing every two days at noon, a total of thirty hours in a month of thirty days. The total is three hundred and sixty hours in a twelve-month period, which is called a day in Heaven Circulation. To find the hour of Heaven Circulation, one begins at midnight on the first day of the year of tzo, the second year, and the month of tzo, ending on the hour of shi, the twelfth hour, of the third day, a total of thirty-six hours. This is called the hour of Heaven Circulation.

The scripture says "the moon comes out from gen" (the west, the White Tiger), which indicates the time for the hour of Heaven Circulation. If the practitioner has not received the true teaching, he will not know that when the moon comes on the third day that it is time to collect the medicine. Only with this knowledge can he learn the secret of the union of the tigers and the dragons. After the third day, the medicine becomes part of his body. On the thirtieth day, the moon wanes, and on the first day the moon returns to the upper corner.

In Heaven, the moon and the sun shoot their powers at each other on the thirtieth and the first days. Because of this, the grand yin (first day) is influenced and conceived through the power of the sun. On the second day the moon and sun rise and set in unison. This phenomenon continues until sunset of the third day, when the moon rises as an eyebrow in the west (the side of the gen). The gen is the gold of tu (the maiden, the eighth trigram of the I Ching) and is going to become the gold of chen (the ninth trigram of the I Ching, the truest and strongest). The moon returns to the southwestern side of the Kuan (the mother, the receptive) and changes into the maiden. From this time the practitioner who seeks the great medicine must wait two ho (one-hour periods), beginning at midnight on the thirtieth day of his innate physical condition (biological rhythm), the midnight of his internal rhythm. He can use this method to identify the exact, appropriate hour of the day, using the next two hours for practice—a total of four hours including the waiting period. After this, the practitioner should wait another two hours, which makes six hours from his internal midnight. During the first four hours, the practitioner should observe the trivet's face, watching to see her lips become purple and her face crimson red, with some soft light between her eyebrows. When the trivet's fluid is exhausted, her eyes shine with light. This is the exact time for creating the medicine. The scripture says that one should calculate with great care the moment when the fluid reaches the second fifth of its cycle, when the eyes reflect light like the scales of a fish, which symbolizes good fortune.

Part III

The Secrets of
Collecting Truth

BUILDING THE FOUNDATION

Firmly secure the essence of Yin
This way you build the foundation
Building the foundation means
Protecting your female [receptive qualities]

Retaining receptivity and avoiding distraction
This is strong guarding
Strongly guard the essence of Yin,
Oh! This is the way you build the foundation
To build the foundation
You must maintain your own female, restrain your male

Maintain your receptivity
Oh! Once you can forcefully retain your essence of Yin
The days until completion of your foundation
Can be counted on your fingers

Oh! What to remember?
As soon as the wind begins to blow
The sail of the boat must be lowered.
Filled to the brim with water, the bottle must be held erect.

COLLECTING THE MEDICINE

*Once you have established the foundation
You can study immortality.
To study immortality,
You must acquire the potion.*

*Only with a strong foundation
Can you harvest the true potion.
Oh! Once your foundation is firmly established,
You may study immortality,
Because Dan Tien (the field of medicine) is
the core of your foundation.*

*Do not waste or exhaust your true mercury,
Search for one who has the true potion,
From whom you may harvest the medicine
Which can help you become a deity.
But first you must build a foundation,
Only then may you harvest the medicine.*

*The medicine will not come to you by itself,
It may only be harvested through effort.
Alas! Do not talk in empty words.
While a host has wine to share
He can send a messenger to invite guests.
A merchant short of capital
Cannot possibly carry on his business!*

KNOWING THE TIME

When will the medicine be generated?
You must know this.

Only if you know can you truly match
The East (Blue Dragon) and the West (White Tiger).
When the East and the west are not matched,
The medicine will not be generated.

When will the medicine be generated?
You must know this.

To generate the medicine is
To generate the potion.

The medicine is generated at a specific time.
If you calculate the right time,
You can acquire true medicine.

The potion, drawn from its source,
Enters and strengthens your mercury.

During the union of East and west,
The pill will naturally take form.

Without true union,
Incomplete Yin or Yang will trouble you.
Oh! Wait patiently, until the moon pays her visit,

The golden flower exudes its beauty,
the Tide swells up, and
its water flows over the beach.

1

STRUMMING THE LUTE

Stroking the bamboo will make it straight
enough to strum the lute

The strumming of the lute and the stroking of bamboo
produce a delightful melody

Until the melody is produced
The bamboo should be stroked without pause

Stroking the bamboo will make it straight
enough to strum the lute

As the bamboo is stroked
My mind becomes empty

Strumming the lute
Teases her organ

As mine teases hers,
It brings her substance to visit
And a delightful clear melody can be heard.
Oh! What must I remember?

Unless the string is taut
The arrow cannot be released from the bow

Unless the wind begins to blow
You cannot sail your boat.

FACING YOUR ENEMY

In battle,
You must allow your opponent to show her ferocity.
For her to be aggressive and active
You must abandon thoughts of heroic action.

Unless all thoughts of heroism are abandoned,
The battle ebbs and flows.

In battle,
She must be encouraged to be expressive.

Battle is a confrontation.
When you engage in this,
Never underestimate your enemy.

This directive is to allow her
To initiate action in intercourse.

You must remain motionless,
For if you move,
You lose your priceless treasure.

Oh! Disallow all carelessness
For if you try to overwhelm your partner,
You overwhelm yourself.
You lose control,
You lose to your opponent.

UPSIDE DOWN

Through practice in the upside-down pose
Straight movement may be achieved.

This straight movement
Brings perfect union to both.
Perfect union is achieved
In the upside-down pose.

Practice in the upside-down pose,
Straight movement may be achieved.

In the pose of upside down
Earth [the female] is above,
Heaven [the male] below.

The pose of upside down
Reverses the normal way.

The normal way allows only
Ordinary practice.

The path to immortality
Requires reversing the normal way.

Ordinary practice leads to
A pit of fire.

Reversing the ordinary way
Transforms one into a deity

With a golden aura.

Upside down, once and again,
The pose produces perfect union.

Oh! You should learn to arrange your partner
On top of you so that the substance of
the East (Earth, the feminine)
May come over to the West (Heaven, the male).

4

In All Sincerity

As you prepare
To collect the potion,
And to become a holy man,
Pray in complete sincerity.

Send your mercury
To meet the true potion,
Begin this endeavor
In complete sincerity.

When your mercury
Meets the true potion,
But cannot blend with it,
In vain, you will hope
To become a holy man.

As you prepare
To collect the true potion
And to become a holy man
You must pray in all sincerity.

Preparing to become a holy man
This is the goal of every practitioner.
The true potion becomes one's true
And unsullied inherent Qi.

As you prepare for the true
And unsullied inherent Qi
To be infused into your own body,
You must purify your mind

And keep it in all sincerity.
You must send your Qi of mercury
From the point where the anus contracts.
Always use concentrated effort
During this contraction.

Oh! Remember!

The Blue Dragon doesn't have to seek
The White Tiger
The Tiger will come to meet the Blue Dragon.

WATER WHEEL

When you have harvested the essence of Yang,
You can claim that you have received the potion.

When you have gathered the true potion,
You can ascend to Heaven.

Eighty-one times, up and down to Heaven,
The true essence becomes your own.

When you have harvested the essence of Yang,
You can claim to have received the potion.

Once you have gathered it,
It is forever yours.
The essence of Yang
Is the true and unsullied inherent Qi—
The gold of water.

When one receives this,
He receives the pure potion.

The practitioner sends his Qi of mercury
Up his back, and down his front.

His Qi is stored in the Ni Wan (brain).

This is the ascending Heaven.

By circulating eighty-one times,
The Golden Elixir will be produced
Oh! To begin the work of ascending Heaven,
You must spin the water wheel
The gold in the water will be drawn up naturally.

THE GATEWAY OF BELIEF

On the crown of the head one may observe
A gateway of belief,
The gateway of the head, a tunnel for
The messenger of the mind to come and go.

On the head of the Blue Dragon, the gateway
Delivers messages of water (Kan) or fire (Li).

On the crown of the head one may observe
A gateway of belief.

The gateway of belief is
The gateway of the head.

The Blue Dragon is the practitioner.
The Tide is regular, like the exact hour
When the gateway occurs and belief arises.

The pearl of red water (the Qi of mercury)
Will descend through the gateway [a word
sometimes translated as labia minor]

Oh! A string of jade
Droops from the nostrils
Of the practitioner.
A shiny golden ball
Grows on the crown of his head.

FOLLOWING OR REVERSING

Heaven (the male) above Earth (the female)
becomes
Earth above Heaven.

Using the pose of Earth above Heaven,
You can become a deity.

The life of a deity can be
As long-lasting as Heaven and Earth.

Heaven above Earth
becomes
Earth above Heaven.

Heaven above Earth,
This condition is unstable.

Earth above Heaven,
This condition is stable.

Following one's usual habits
Brings unstable conditions.

Reversing one's usual habits
Brings stable conditions.

Simply following your instinct,
You create another ordinary being.

Reversing your instincts,
You will become a holy man.

If you don't use the pose
Of Earth above Heaven,
How can you become a deity?

Once you reach the level of a deity,
You will enjoy the longevity of Heaven.

Ah! I will see you in Heaven.
These teachings will shine between Heaven and Earth
Rarely spoken by man, either ancient or today—
The teachings of my school.

Part IV

The Way of Gathering the Truth

PREPARING FOR FURTHER ENGAGEMENT

Focus your mind on the essence of Yin
Do not let your mind think about external affairs

Like a mountain you sit in tranquility
For fifty days,

Day and night you maintain your vigil,
Your mind focused on your Dan Tien

When at last the fluids are released from your heart and kidneys
and blend well,
You will be freed from bondage.

When your Qi and blood circulate perfectly
Your beauty is enhanced.
Once your body and spirit attain this mystical condition,
You become a superior man.

Relaxing yourself, you enter the state of void,
You will receive messages which come from your Ni Wan (brain)
and Yu Zen (the base of the skull).

Then you will constantly feel the flow
from the two sides of your spinal acupoints.

Gradually you must extend your study beyond
control of your nostril and mouth breathing.

At the critical moment, you should know
To contract your anus.

Armed with my teaching, you will have no difficulty
In building your foundation.

When the time is right, you may proceed
To unite the Male and Female.

Do you understand? This describes building the foundation for practice, and waiting until the time is right. When the wind begins to blow, the sail of the boat must be lowered. When the bottle is erect, its water will reach its upper rim. You must firmly retain your essence of Yin, your body's most precious treasure. You must be removed from the world and live in a quiet room. You must undertake this one hundred-day practice, without wasting time, in constant awareness of your need to blend the fluids of your heart and kidney. When the woman's water flows and her fire ebbs, she will raise her body forward and send her message—then you must pull her closer to you and drink from her fountain. At this moment, you control your breath and contract your anus, then enter into a trance. This is not yet the highest level of mystery, and you should not be surprised if your soul leaves your body. You can now achieve the impossible feats described in the poems, without losing your true mercury. At the critical moment you must collect the lid to produce the medicine. The amount is about one cupful.

In my estate, pure wine is stored.
From the west pond
In solitude, I drink.

This explains the passage in the poem from page 68, "If you have wine to share, you can send messengers to invite guests. If you are short of capital, how can you carry out your business?" Even when you know you have accumulated sufficient substance, you must still wait for just the right moment. You must safeguard your mercury, carefully, without losing it. You have consistently worked to build your foundation and to maintain a receptive demeanor, without showing your male character, all for this purpose. Anticipating the time when you will become a deity, you must not only store up your mercury, you must seek the true medicine. Before you collect the true medicine, you must build up a strong foundation. Once your foundation becomes strong, you may undertake the procedure to collect the medicine, and make it your own. The way to learn to become a deity is this simple.

A flute without holes
Doesn't need to be held horizontally.
It is blown randomly
The air that passes through
It flows and moves something inside.
Thus wind is generated and gathered
On top of the head of the meditator.

I discuss the "The Tiger Blows the Flute"—arranging a girl to sit in front of the meditator. The girl should be a qualified consort. Before the flute is blown, air will not enter it. If the air doesn't enter it, the channel is not open, and the elixir will not move. The practitioner can't blow it himself. He has to ask others to blow it, and make the channel open so the elixir can pass through it. Then the practitioner can use the elixir for refinement. If he feels there is wind generated and gathered on the top of his head, this is the sign of the effectiveness of correctly blowing the flute.

THE SONG OF WIND IN THE FLUTE

Thirteen, then twenty-five
Accompanied by thirty-seven.

Forty and nine
Followed by fifty-one.

Sixty-three,
Then seventy-five.

Eighty-one is reached,
Ninety-seven should be done.

One hundred is attained,
Return to seven.

Seventeen Poems of the True Secret

Poem 1

With chests touching and her legs on top,
Her emotions are aroused.

Arms embracing and holding shoulders,
She feels excitement.

This is the true mystical way
To strum the lute.

Melodious sounds can be produced
Without using unclean hands.

Explanation

The dragon strums the tiger's lute, with her legs above him, to excite her emotions. Again, embracing her, holding her arms, and holding her shoulders brings her excitement. When she is aroused, the melodious sounds will be created. When she reaches complete arousal, mystical events will occur. This is called "strumming the stringless lute thoroughly brings clear sounds from within." It is most important to simply enjoy strumming the lute, without concentrating on the sound.

Striking the bamboo, my organ dances. Strumming the lute, hers is aroused. Striking my organ and arousing hers naturally produces melodious sounds. There is a saying, "When the melodious sounds have not come, you must strike the bamboo. Striking the bamboo, and maintaining its erectness, allows you to strum the lute." Beware, for this is not for simple amusement. When the string of the bow remains loose, you must not send your arrow. When the wind begins to blow, you must lower the sail of the boat.

POEM 2

The dragon seizes the tiger first.
The tiger seizes the dragon later.

The dragon clasps the tiger
and the tiger clasps the dragon,
This enhances their arousal.

At this moment, the dragon begins to practice,
Following the verbal instructions of the master.

All the master's verbal instructions should be
Diligently carried out.

Explanation

When the dragon clasps the tiger, this should be with the dragon's organ pointing upwards and the tiger's downward. This is the standard pose for arranging a stable consort. Her arms encircle you, and yours encircle her. This is like two Chinese characters "seven" arranged with one backwards. The practice in this verse has revealed more techniques than previous verses. I will reveal more secret words in the verses that follow.

POEM 3

Initiation to the secret words can occur
only from mouth to mouth.
Also, the secret word initiation
leads to a mystical path,
In which the practitioner can foresee
the arousal of the fire,
And the radiation of its light.
At this time he introduces the Blue Dragon
to arouse the mystical potion.

Explanation

The practice of the union of the dragon and the tigers transforms the human body internally. The heart of the human is the lord of the body. The meridians of the small intestine and the tongue connect with the heart, which allows the entanglement of the two tongues to enhance the prosperity of the heart's flare. When the flare of the heart prospers, the small intestine swells. Then the practitioner can foresee the coming of the primordial true potion. When the practitioner receives the true potion, the true initiation to the secret words is revealed to him.

POEM 4

To arouse her feelings
The Blue Dragon is brought out
To meet with the black turtle.

The luster of the pearl glitters
Through the curtain

If the head of the Blue Dragon
Hasn't been presented
How can you hear the explosion
of the earthen thunder
in the Gate of Heaven?

Explanation

The dragon must become a fire dragon; then he can seize the tiger. The Gate of Heaven means the northwestern direction. The earthen thunder refers to the 24th hexagram of the I Ching, Fu, which means return [In this hexagram the thunder is in the womb of the Earth.] When the essence of Yang is generated in the northwest, the practitioner presents the Blue Dragon to arouse the black turtle. This is called "When the Yang initiates an action, water drains from the consort at midnight." The consort's warm luster glitters through the curtain.

POEM 5

Bringing out the dragon to seize the tiger,
The practitioner's action leads to another result.
At this moment, the Earth should reverse its position
to become Heaven.

Further mystical excitement of acting upside down,
If you are curious to know.

To explore the edge of the partner's tongue,
This is the true secret.

Explanation

The tiger of the Earth and the dragon of Heaven must reverse their positions to the upside-down position. Presenting the dragon to seize the tiger is the technique for arousing the partner's emotions. To practice the position upside down, and upside down again, this is to anticipate a result. The practitioner wishes his internal fire to transfer to the head of the dragon. He also uses the secret words to lick his partner's tongue, and from the edge of the partner's tongue he hears the partner's clear sound and witnesses the true secret. When the Earth is arranged above Heaven, the practitioner proceeds to lick the heart of the partner's tongue. The tongue becomes as hot as fire, and afterwards it becomes damp, producing moisture. The practitioner should then begin the next movement. He must send the dragon to abide in the cave of the tiger, and the tiger should come to meet the dragon. The tiger should act and the dragon should match its movement. When the tiger's tongue is as hot as fire, the practitioner should be aware her Tide is coming. When the tiger's tongue is as cold as ice, he should know that is the moment the essence of Yang is generating. Abiding in the cave of the tiger, the practitioner can achieve a great feat. This is very important indeed!

POEM 6

Abiding in the cave of the tiger,
The dragon enjoys the same excitement as the tiger.

At this moment, the dragon makes his endeavor
With all his breath.

Maintaining the upside-down position,
The tiger starts to wiggle or jump.

A drop of fluid drains suddenly,
Reaching the place of my eastern part.

Explanation

While the dragon abides in the cave of the tiger, the dragon stays above and the tiger beneath. While the dragon enters the gate of the tiger, the tiger is the dragon's guest. These are the practices of ordinary people. If the dragon instead becomes the guest of the tiger, this is the way of practicing the Tao. The practitioner firmly restrains his emotions, and uses his mind to guide his Qi for circulation at the critical moment. If the practitioner cannot maintain the discipline for this practice, he can never achieve this desirable feat.

POEM 7

Whether she reaches her peak of excitement
I do not know.

Patiently waiting,
I keep my mind empty.

When she bows down her head, and closes her eyes,
It is time for the true potion to come.

In a flash, it passes,
Like the spark which becomes a flame.

Explanation

The dragon asks the tiger how she feels; whether she is happy, I do not know. I ask, then she replies. If she continues bowing down her head and closing her eyes, I inhale deeply through my nose. I practice this art. Who else would know what I am doing? And the effectiveness of this practice happens as quickly as a fire ignites from a spark.

POEM 8

The tiger of the west comes out
To meet the Blue Dragon.

The tiger cannot imagine that the dragon
has opened his eastward channel.

Inhaling deeply, the dragon holds the tiger
and does not release her.

This achievement, this marvelous feat,
Can be attained only through this practice.

Explanation

The tiger jumps into the lake of the dragon, making an upside-down movement. The tiger comes out to meet the Blue Dragon; the tiger cannot imagine the dragon capturing the tiger. The dragon uses his nose to inhale and draw in the potion, and lets it trace up the channel along the spine. As the potion comes forth it behaves like a pearl of fire. The dragon must practice the art of Heaven's ascending boat. If you haven't learned this art from your instructor, do not substitute any other practice, for this could lead to dangerous results. If you have already received this instruction, then its effectiveness is immediate.

POEM 9

The potion is transferred to my eastern side,
I stretch out my leg and use my hands to pull.

If I don't stretch and pull,
My essence will escape my control.

Once I've practiced for a certain time,
I have sufficient energy.

I let it flow naturally
and pass through my Wei Lu gate (tailbone acupoint)

Explanation

The tiger's essence is coming, so the dragon starts stretching his legs, his feet pointing heavenward. Again he uses both hands to hold the back of his thighs, to stretch them. This verse reveals a new addition to the practice of the dragon. I introduce these many practices for the cultivation of the body and the mind, all preparation is for this purpose. Without preparatory practice, how can the practitioner receive the potion and have it transfer into his body, and become fused with his own?

POEM 10

It is clear that they appear as two bodies,
Man and woman.
Actually, the Li (fire, man) is not a man.
The Kan (water, woman) is not a woman.

Though Kan (water, woman) has a female form,
Her body holds a male essence.

A man has a male's form,
His body holds a female essence.

Do not blame the guest
Who becomes the host in your home.

You must learn the way of
Becoming a guest at the right moment.

Though Heaven above must
Rotate to become the Earth

Kuan, the humble Earth,
Will become Heaven (Chen).

Two bodies have different essences,
Each hoping to acquire the substance of the other.

Yin and Yang entangle to exchange,
The struggle to get the other's essence is merciless.

In the chamber, you are in tranquil meditation
Diligently you practice, and with a relaxed mind, you enjoy it.

You arrange your chamber to be simple and clean,
You aspire with all sincerity to reach your goal.

When you enter the gate
You must learn to be gentle and unhurried.

When you enter the door
You must remain unhurried.

Throughout this time, you must restrain your emotions,
Do not let them become aroused to a dangerous level.

Through these methods you have the opportunity
To mingle Yin and Yang in perfect union.

Explanation

This is the basic practice. The practitioner must know that through the union of the man and woman, he can actually achieve his goal. The Kan and the Li are terms of the parable. The practitioner has a bodily form of Yang, but his inner essence is pure Yin. The woman inherits a bodily form of Yin, though her inner essence is absolute Yang. The practitioner has to exchange his pure Yin essence with the absolute essence of Yang. He has to borrow this Yang from a female's bodily form, and the procedure for achieving this relies on the practice of upside-down exchange. The practitioner must focus on his goal, without losing his concentration or dozing off. In an unhurried manner, he enters the cave. With full earnestness of endeavor, he slowly retreats. Without extreme hurry or delay, this practice can be repeated and continued.

POEM 11

If you ask me about the details of the procedure,
I would say that the practice is not too difficult.

All achievement can be completed
In a brief period of time.

You lie on the ground
And you visualize your goal.

You bend your knees and
Use your hands to pull them close to your chest.

While the pill traces the length of the channel,
Do not let it be stopped.

The water wheel is moving,
Do not let it stop.

If you can climb to the summit eighty-one times
Without losing your concentration,

This substance will be able to turn
And pass over the curve.

After it passes over the curve,
It still has a long way to go.

Quickly you sit up
And straighten your spine.

Holding still, raise up and contract your anus.
This is the correct method.

Once again, place your hands on each side of your loins
This is the right pose to adopt.

Inhale
While the Qi moves up your spine

Separate the Yin and the Yang.
Pressing your lips against your teeth, you use your strength.

If you do not respect this method,
and waste your body's strength

How is it possible
To acquire the delicious food to taste?

Explanation

This describes the procedure of endeavor. How to receive the potion from the other person? You must concentrate deeply on the circumstances. Lying on the ground, you use your two hands to encircle your knees and those of your consort, pulling them to your chest, and pounding them against it. If you can climb to the summit eighty-one times, you can receive the substance naturally, the essence of Yang. Once you have captured the essence of Yang, the potion becomes your own. You smile at her, she smiles at you. The channel for the pill is unobstructed. And your mind is free of random thoughts. You begin to guide your Qi to circulate like a water wheel turning water in the river. Your organ is constantly erect, and you must inhale and constantly imagine drawing in [the potion]. Oh! When you are climbing to the summit, you must sit up. When you start the water wheel, the water will be drawn up in a circular movement, and when you realize that this substance has passed beyond the curve, you must sit up immediately. You straighten your spine and contract your anus and put your hands on the sides of your loins. Do not let the substance go downward. If you wish this substance to move up your spine, you must inhale. If you wish to break your Yin and Yang connection, you must use your strength by pressing your lips against your teeth. The potion then comes down to your throat and enters your lower abdomen, and the erection of your organ is slightly reduced. If you can achieve this feat, you can clap your hands and burst into a great laugh.

POEM 12

When the potion approaches my body,
I do not know it in advance.

I only feel the potion as it enters
And, like a ball of fire, it runs and rolls.

She loses the potion,
And it comes to me and infuses my body

As soon as the potion is released from her body,
I initiate the preparatory work.

If the potion is truly generated
My action is meaningful.

If the potion is not made,
I pull my knees and raise my inhalation in vain.

Before pulling knees and raising the inhalation
You must be certain the potion is coming.

When the potion comes to me,
I hurry to pull up my knees.

Lightly I use five-ninths of my energy to pull up my knees
With three inhalations and three exhalations.

Heavily I raise up my knees using nine-ninths of my power
With three inhalations and three exhalations

The potion passes over my Wei Lu [tailbone acupoint]
And flows along my spine.

Further along it hits my Yu Zen [the base of the skull]
And comes to the Ni Wan [brain]

Eventually it reaches
The summit of my crown.

How can it come down from there?
Does it need a ladder for this?

I inhale in my throat and suck in mucous fluid
In order to draw it down.

I stick two fingers in my nostrils
To prevent it from seeping out the outlets.

For a moment I cease all effort,
And the potion drops into my mouth.

Motionless for a while,
I feel it flow down into my throat.

With a swallow of saliva,
The potion runs down into my Dan Tien.

There it will be nourished for ten months,
And a holy fetus forms.

Explanation

When the potion reaches you, you use the method of pulling the knees and pounding on the chest. When the potion starts to trace up your body, you must sit up with your knees folded for meditation. Use five-ninths of your energy to pull and draw in your knees. Use nine-ninths of your energy to raise them up and let it ascend your spine. Oh! Who can see there is something ascending in my body? Like a person who drinks water, whether it is cold or hot, only he can know this.

Travel on water is easy and smooth. Travel over hills is difficult and tiresome. On the summit of the head, there is a gate of merit. When the partner's merit is collected, we send it to this gate. Then it will descend as if walking down a ladder to the throat. Therefore there is a saying, "Once it reaches the Li Wan, a party can be prepared to celebrate. After it reaches the Thon Lo [throat], one may accept congratulations as being an immortal."

When the potion comes to Li Wan, it has to descend to the Dan Tien. It comes to the Dan Tien, where it lingers and enters the crevices of the region of the Dan Tien. "The nostrils drip two jades, the crown of the head wears a golden ball." This feat awaits you. You inhale mucous fluid in your throat to draw down the potion. Then you stick two fingers into your nostrils to prevent the potion escaping. You anticipate the potion as it drops into your throat, and remain motionless for a while. Then you feel your head is growing a horn, and you are glad of this. Afterwards, you must learn the art of kindling and quenching a fire for ten months.

POEM 13

Three tigers worship the dragon
and nourish him with water.
The ceremony should be conducted without interruption.

Two of them are chosen.
One is used at the Chun (3rd hexagram)
The other is the Meng (4th hexagram).

These two hexagrams are used
To continue the ceremony in the morning and evening.

One tiger should be cautious,
The scarlet flower blossoms monthly.

Explanation

Three tigers worship the dragon. One tiger is caught with the monthly affair. The other two play the roles of Chun and Meng. They are virgins, inherently pure essence of Yang. This explains why a consort [trivet] must have three legs. In the morning, one of the girls is chosen, and in the evening, the other. If they happen to meet the period of scarlet flowers blossoming, the third can be substituted. In the beginning, the rotation starts from the 3rd (Chun) and 4th hexagram (Meng), at the end the 2nd hexagram

(Kuan) meets with the 64th hexagram (Wei-Ji) in rotation. The practitioner continues the procedure until six hundred hexagrams have been adopted.

POEM 14

The scarlet flowers blossom monthly,
The gold comes to visit every month.

The gold can be captured
One day before it comes to visit.

While the gold disappears with the scarlet flower
The jade flower will blossom.

The dancing pollen of the jade flower appears
This is the true menstruation.

Explanation

The practitioner begins the procedure of collecting the gold continuously for the purpose of watering. The moment when the potion is generated should be known. When you know the specific time, you can arrange to blend East and West together. If you don't know the time, trouble may occur—the flower blossoms. Be cautious of the stirring of the Tide. When the Tide comes, the golden flower will appear at the same time. When the Tide comes, the water flows up the beach. Do not pluck the golden flower which has faded. You must collect the fresh jade pollen which has just bloomed. This jade pollen has a flavor as sweet as the spring and smooth as cream. When the true moment comes, the tiger looks like a full moon, and has brilliant light. When you look at the radiant moon, you know that the true moment is coming. Its coming has neither form nor shadow. But the practitioner can sense and feel it.

Poem 15

Then you know that
you can fully dominate your fate

What you should do now is
To seek those who can nourish you with water

Later on you continue the practice
of blowing the holeless flute

And strum the lute
but not on another's body

Seamlessly be hidden
The string of lute in your stomach

Carefully be guarded
Your mind focused on this place

All things in the world
Are forgettable and unimportant

Deliberately thinking
Only this is the gold in your eyes.

Explanation

Do not think that once you have received the potion, you can discontinue all practice. After you receive the potion, you need to transplant it in the pond of potion, where it receives the constant dripping from above, and you use mild fire (Wen Fou) and strong fire (Wu Fou) to heat it from below. Every month you must do this procedure once. So it is called nourishment with water. Continue this practice for ten months, and do not omit the work of heating. From this introduction, you can see that for a practitioner to nourish and generate an elixir, he must learn many crafts. I tell you to continue blowing the holeless flute and strum the stringless lute. This is absolutely right. To enhance the flame of the fire, blow it when the wind blows. To push a boat, follow the direction of the current of the water. You must hide the stringless lute in your stomach, and focus it carefully from time to time.

POEM 16

There are six hundred verses
To depict the work of nourishment with water.

Each verse seems similar
Describing the way to collect the true potion.

At the hour of midnight [hour of tze] you kindle the fire
And maintain the upside-down pose.

At noon [the hour of wu] you reduce the fire
To maintain a certain temperature
You practice the upside-down pose again.

As soon as your spine touches the ground
You feel a fire is lit and blown by the wind.

It seems to ascend on the back of your body
then descend along the front of your chest.

Ten months with this practice
Your training is good and sufficient
Again, facing the wall
You sit and meditate there for nine years.

Explanation

Nourishment with water, to keep it warm for ten months, this is like conceiving a baby. Six hundred verses, we talked about using two hexagrams a day, Chun and Meng, and ten months have three hundred days, therefore six hundred hexagrams must be used. You must kindle (send in) the fire at midnight, and reduce it at noon. However, the fire is generated at the hour of ten p.m. [the hour of yen] and its flame quenched at the hour of two a.m. [the hour of wu]. Noon and midnight are not the only times you may practice this. All hours in the evening and the morning you can practice the upside-down pose, and meet with the principle of Yin and Yang [at twelve-hour intervals]. However, the living hour of midnight and noon [ho tze wu shi], the hour of mau, six p.m. and nine p.m., the hour of yen, mild fire (Wen Fou) and strong fire (Wu Fou) and perpetual warmth, I can't explain these in detail; you must wait to ask your own instructor. Most people in the world are scandalized by my teaching. I just smile and laugh at their ignorance.

This is the practice in which the dragon has intercourse with twelve tigers. First you command a qualified consort to blow the flute so that the Qi can enter and flow through the mystical channel. Then you hold each other close with your legs crossed and hook your arms on each other's shoulders and around your arms, to arouse her emotions. Each of you is delighted to become the other's captive.

You use your tongue to lick her tongue to make her heart's flame increase, and her small intestine will distend. Her face will radiate a reddish luster, like a precious pearl. Again you tease and arouse her emotions, then her first essence of Yang is generated and her true potion is coming. You arrange her to sit on top of you, using your tongue to lick the center of her tongue. You use your dragon to explore the cave of the tiger. If the tongue of the tiger is as cold as ice and the head of the dragon is hot as fire you order her to act, but you stay motionless. If you act, then you cannot overwhelm her, hence my past master says "when in war you have to let her become ferocious." She is ferocious but I do not show my heroic character, namely, if you assault others you assault yourself. Once you have lost yourself, you lose your partner. If her emotions are aroused to the highest peak, her physical body reaches the hour of living midnight [ho tze shi]. She lowers her head and closes her eyes. In her mouth accumulates abundant sweet dew, and you use your tongue to guide the dew into your mouth. Then you inhale deeply through your nose, which will open the channel along your spine. Also, when you inhale, the potion will come to you like a kindled fire pearl. Inside the stove, the temperature is high, and the heat of the head of the dragon has a strong flame. You point your two feet towards Heaven, and use your two hands to hold the back of your thighs and stretch them with your full strength. Once more you pull your knees and the woman back towards your chest. In the beginning you do this lightly, later you can do this more forcefully. When you have received the true potion, you have to separate from her, and sit up. The true potion flies over the Wei Lu acupoint (the tailbone), and you contract your anus as if you were holding a stool, and then inhale your mucous fluid and clench your teeth and lips together. Inhale gently when you lift up the potion, counting eighty-one times, then enhance the inhalation with heavy breath, and transform the potion, also eighty-one times. The potion passes over the Wei Lu, Jia Ji (middle of the spine), and Yu Zen (the base of the skull), and reaches the Ni Wan (the brain). Then you place two fingers into your nostrils and inhale the mucous fluid into your throat. You feel that some kind of fluid is generated in your brain and you visualize it dripping down, and you swallow it into your throat. The two things meet and blend together. You make a tranquil meditation, concentrating on storing your spirit and regulating your Qi. In this way your spirit and your Qi are in unity.

POEM 17

As you anticipate receiving the potion
You must pray in all sincerity.

In all sincerity
You send your mercury (the Qi of your blood)
to meet with the potion.

When they meet but cannot blend together
You anticipate in vain.

As you anticipate receiving the true potion,
You must pray in all sincerity.

Explanation

The innate true potion will come to your body and you will be able to receive it only if you are truly sincere. With complete sincerity, you contract your anus, and send your true mercury to meet with it. The effort should be measured and exact. If the effort is too great or too small, you may not achieve your goal. It is important to be very careful. The dragon doesn't have to seek the White Tiger; the tiger will seek the dragon. The practitioner must sit well to regulate his breath, guide his Qi, and fortify his sperm so that his Qi (in his blood) can circulate well in his body, and his mind and body reach a perfectly tranquil condition. Therefore during the one hundred days, the practitioner lives in a quiet chamber, practicing carefully the art of controlling his breath, contracting his anus, stretching and pulling his thighs, and guiding the potion up and down.

When this technique reaches maturity, the practitioner will not plunge into confusion at the important moment. Before he practices five thousand and forty-eight hours, he can practice for a period of thirty hours. Through this practice he can train his mind, transform his character, and control his sperm, forging his mystical sword, nourish his kidneys' fluid (water) and his heart's heat (fire), saliva, the Qi of his blood. He can learn the art of raising and lowering, transporting, lifting, swallowing, and delivery. At the calculated time, the practitioner faces the woman. He strikes the bamboo and strums the lute, has intercourse and has Heaven and Earth in perfect union. When the tail of the White Tiger wiggles and trembles, the head of the Blue Dragon is erect and straight. When the cave of the woman opens and closes, the root of Heaven is raised and erect. The root of Heaven raises erect again and again as the cave of the moon opens and closes repeatedly. At the same time, the tiger's tail is raised and erect, and its cave clasps again and again. During these contractions, no man can prevent his sea of sperm from being aroused. When the fluid swells up and surrounds the head of the dragon, it almost shocks and numbs. This critical moment feels like one is standing against a current of raging water, and he must clench his teeth, close his eyes, and stop his ears. Closing his mouth and using nostril breathing, he inhales, and contracts his anus. Then he stops breathing, and all the orifices of his body are shut down.

He can caress the tiger's buttocks, grasp her breasts, and suck her tongue, embrace her waist, straighten her knees, as the dragon clasps its legs and sends in his fire, concentrating his thoughts. The dragon pushes the tiger to give up its potion, and orders the tiger to act and lets the tiger wiggle and be released. When the tiger reaches her highest emotion, her gold will float up. When you see the tiger embracing the dragon's waist and lower her head and close her eyes, the fluid starts to drain down. When the tiger's tongue is as cold as ice, the sweet dew is generated, and swells up like a fountain, you can instruct her not to swallow it down, and you can use your mouth to receive it. The tiger's tongue is as hot as fire, and the temperature in its stove is like boiling water. The dragon must instruct the tiger to separate, and the dragon draws out his sword, stretches his legs, and holds back his thighs. Concentrating on the practice of the art of the ascending Heaven, you raise your tongue and inhale through your nose. Then, you shrug your shoulders and draw the Qi back, and focus on the Shuan Kwen, the mystical gate (another name for the Dan Tien).

In anticipation of receiving the potion, with all your mind you hold your head erect, straighten your spine, and await the potion's passing over your Wei Lu acupoint, then sit straight and put both hands at your waist. With a deep inhalation, the potion is drawn up to a higher level. You continue the inhalation and bend your back forward, and the potion will penetrate three gates. Then you bow your head suddenly, suck your lips, and the potion will pass over the base of your head at the Yu Zen acupoint. After this, lower your head, and suck your lips and place two fingers into your nostrils. The potion then reaches the summit of the head, with a contracted inhalation. Now make a roar, and inhale the mucous fluid into this roar. The potion drops from the upper palate to the cheeks. You send it with your true mercury gently downward to your throat, and let it meet with the gold fluid which you swallowed down before.

When they both reach your middle chest, you guide them to circulate in meditation. You contain your Qi and swallow your saliva, and your spirit and your Qi are joined in union. This practice can be carried on either forging your character or nourishing you with water. However, when meeting the period for bathing (meditation at six a.m. and six p.m.), you should retreat from the fire, and you can stop practicing this. You just keep your stove warm and nourish it. This art should be carefully nurtured. If you have the luck of reading this book, you should build up your good credit and attributes, and you will have no problems reaching the Tao.

The Laughing Roar

At the end of this book, I write a poem to express my expectations of the Tao.

The twelve girls young and pretty
Know the art of blowing the flute.

If a practitioner has no money
He cannot buy these damsels.

I have sympathy for those who
Devote themselves to the Tao and wish to find the truth.

In solitude they live and meditate
In the quiet and trackless hills.

Blame me not
If you find the art of my sexual practices strange

True or false,
They can be proven over time.

He who knows not that
There is a true cave which was considered false before

Through swift action
It traces the meridian like a swimming dragon.

How profound are the mystical words
Of the Fon Fou Zen Ren (the true men of wind and fire)

In the shadow of the palm tree
I play the lute by the light of the new moon

Suddenly a gust of cool wind blows
The dragon jumps into the deep waters of the lake
And the tiger runs into the forest with a laughing roar.

CPI Antony Rowe
Eastbourne, UK
June 30, 2022